A Taste of the
North Country

Adirondack Regional Recipes

Wendy Harrington
Illustrated by Sheri Amsel

Cover design and illustration by Sheri Amsel

Harrington, Wendy
        A taste of the north country: adirondack regional recipes/
written by Wendy Harrington, illustrated by Sheri Amsel.

Includes Index.
ISBN 0-9741320-0-4

Sheri Amsel
Publication

TABLE OF CONTENTS

4

Muffins, Rolls and Bread

Please don't skip this section even if you don't consider yourself a baker. All of the recipes are very easy to make, and there is nothing as nice as freshly baked treats, unbeatable for breakfast and indispensable for picnics and potlucks.

THE BEST BLUEBERRY MUFFINS makes one dozen

2 cups flour
$^1/_2$ cup sugar
2 teaspoons baking powder
$^1/_2$ teaspoon salt
1 egg, slightly beaten
$^3/_4$ cup milk
$^1/_2$ cup (1 stick) butter, melted
1 cup fresh blueberries
Cinnamon sugar

Preheat oven to 425° and lightly grease and flour a12 cavity muffin pan. In a medium bowl, combine dry ingredients and mix until blended. Add the egg, milk and melted butter, stirring until just moistened.

Fold in the blueberries.

Spoon batter into prepared muffin pan, filling each cavity $^2/_3$ full, and sprinkle tops with cinnamon sugar.

Bake in a 425° oven for 20 to 25 minutes or until golden brown.

APPLE ORCHARD MUFFINS makes one dozen

2 cups flour
1$^1/_2$ teaspoon baking powder
$^1/_2$ teaspoon salt
$^1/_4$ cup shortening
1 egg, slightly beaten
1 cup milk
3 medium apples
Brown sugar for topping

Preheat oven to 400°, lightly grease 12 medium sized muffin tins. In a medium bowl, combine the dry ingredients, cut in the shortening until mixture is crumbly. Add the egg and milk, stir until blended. Drop dough evenly into the 12 prepared tins.

Peel and core the apples, cut each apple into quarters. Lightly press apple piece onto dough, one per muffin, core side up. Sprinkle the apple with brown sugar.

Bake at 400° for 25 minutes, until dough is browned and apple is slightly tender.

Remove from tins, and allow to cool slightly.

DROP HAM AND CHEESE BISCUITS

makes one dozen

This is a great recipe for breakfast on the go, these can be start to finish in about 15 minutes and they reheat well.

2 cups flour
$^1/_4$ teaspoon salt
1 teaspoon baking powder
1 tablespoon fresh chives, cut into small pieces or 1 tablespoon dried chives
$^1/_3$ cup vegetable oil
$^2/_3$ cup milk
$^1/_2$ cup shredded sharp Cheddar cheese
$^1/_2$ cup finely diced, cooked ham

Preheat oven to 475°. Lightly grease a 12 cavity cupcake pan. In a medium bowl, combine dry ingredients and chives, mix to combine. Stir in oil and milk, stirring just until ingredients are combined.

Add cheese and ham, blend lightly.

Spoon batter evenly into prepared pan and bake at 475° for 10 to 12 minutes, until puffy and browned.

Remove from pan and serve.

If you want to do these as an appetizer, use a 24 cavity mini muffin tin and bake for 6 to 8 minutes.

BACKPACKER'S BANNOCK

makes one 12 inch round 'loaf'

A traditional trail bread and a family favorite, you don't have to be on a mountaintop to enjoy this easy bread, great with chili or stew. When you are hiking along and stumble onto a patch of wild berries, add a bit more sugar and use it for a delicious trailside shortcake.

$1^1/_2$ cups flour
2 teaspoons baking powder
2 teaspoons sugar (double this amount for shortcake)
2 tablespoons powdered milk
1 tablespoon vegetable oil
$^3/_4$ cup water
2 tablespoons butter

Combine all the ingredients except the water and butter, mix well. Place into a quart sized recloseable bag.

To prepare the bannock, melt 2 tablespoons butter in a cast iron skillet over medium high heat.

If you are using an open campfire, bring the butter to a sizzle so you know the pan is hot enough.

Add $^3/_4$ cup water to the bag, close it and squish it around with your hands until well blended. Empty the bag into the pan, spreading the dough evenly.

Cook for 8 to 10 minutes on each side, don't let it brown too much and use a straw to test the inside.

When done, remove from heat and cut into wedges to serve.

SKILLET CORNBREAD serves 10

The best cornbread has great corn flavor, a tender texture and a crispy golden crust. This one has all that, and uses leftover corn cut from the cob, or substitute frozen corn kernels when fresh is out of season.

$^1/_2$ cup (1 stick) butter, softened
$^2/_3$ cup white sugar
$^1/_4$ cup honey
2 eggs
$^1/_2$ teaspoon salt
$1^1/_2$ cups flour
$^3/_4$ cup cornmeal
$^1/_2$ teaspoon baking powder
$^1/_2$ cup milk
$1^1/_2$ cups corn, from the cob or frozen
2 tablespoons butter for skillet

Preheat oven to 425°.

Cream together the butter, sugar, honey, eggs and salt. Mix in the flour, cornmeal and baking powder; blend well. Stir in milk and corn.

Put 2 tablespoons butter in cast iron, or other oven proof skillet. Put in oven for a few minutes until butter is melted and hot, but not browned. When batter is ready, remove skillet from oven and pour in batter, being careful not to splatter the hot butter. Place skillet back in oven and bake for 20 to 25 minutes.

Remove from oven and cut into wedges to serve. You can bake this in a greased 9x13 inch pan, the crust won't be as crispy, but still very tasty.

JALAPENO BEER BREAD makes 1 loaf

Serve this with any camp style meal, a real hit with the hot pepper fans.

3 cups self rising flour
2 tablespoons white sugar
1 can (12 fluid ounces) beer, at room temperature
$^1/_2$ cup shredded Cheddar cheese
$^1/_4$ cup chopped jalapenos, fresh or canned
$^1/_4$ cup ($^1/_2$ stick) butter, melted

Preheat oven to 350° and lightly grease a 9x5 inch loaf pan.

In a large bowl, stir together the flour, sugar, beer, cheese and peppers. The batter will foam a bit as the beer reacts to the self rising flour, the yeast in the beer helps make the whole thing rise. Spoon the batter; it will be quite stiff, into prepared pan, spread evenly. Pour the melted butter evenly over the whole loaf.

Bake for 50 to 60 minutes until a toothpick inserted in bread comes out clean. Hot, as in hot peppers, is a relative thing, add more or use different varieties to suit your taste.

RHUBARB BREAD makes 2 loaves

Rhubarb is one of the easiest crops to grow in my Northern Adirondack garden, and after a long, cold winter, I look forward to anything fresh out of the garden. The popularity of rhubarb has dropped in the last few decades, but I predict a comeback as more people buy regionally produced foods and get great recipes like this one that incorporate great taste with local ingredients.

$1^1/_2$ cups packed light brown sugar
$^2/_3$ cup vegetable oil
1 egg
1 cup sour milk—add 1 T vinegar to 1 C milk and let stand
1 teaspoon vanilla
$2^1/_2$ cups flour
1 teaspoon baking powder
$1^1/_2$ cups tender rhubarb, cut into 1/2 inch pieces
1 cup chocolate chips
$^1/_2$ cup chopped pecans
$^1/_2$ cup raisins

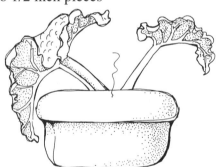

TOPPING:
$^1/_2$ cup white sugar
1 tablespoon butter, melted
1 teaspoon cinnamon

Preheat the oven to 350°. Grease two 9x5 inch loaf pans well. In a large mixing bowl, combine the ingredients in the order given, mixing after each addition.

Spoon the batter equally into the prepared pans. Mix the topping ingredients in a small bowl using a fork until crumbly. Sprinkle evenly over the loaves. Bake for 50 minutes, until toothpick tests clean.

Remove from oven, let cool in pans for 10 minutes before cooling completely on wire rack. This freezes very nicely, so eat one now and freeze one for later.

FALL FESTIVAL PUMPKIN LOAVES makes 2 loaves

Pumpkin is another crop that grows well in this climate. I think of pumpkins as food, not just decorations for the season, easy to store, a cinch to prepare, and a main ingredient for fabulous fall foods.

$^1/_2$ medium pumpkin, seeded, quartered, baked until tender, cooled and mashed OR
2 cups canned pumpkin without added spices
$3^1/_2$ cups flour
2 teaspoons baking soda
$^1/_2$ teaspoon salt
1 teaspoon cinnamon
1 teaspoon nutmeg
3 cups sugar
1 cup vegetable oil
4 eggs
$^2/_3$ cup water
1 cup chopped walnuts

Let the baked pumpkin cool, scoop pulp from peel, mash and measure two cups.

Preheat the oven to 350° and lightly grease two 9x5 inch loaf pans. In a large mixing bowl, mix the dry ingredients together; add the mashed pumpkin, oil, eggs and water, mixing until well blended. Fold in nuts and divide batter evenly between the prepared pans.

Bake for 1 hour, until bread tests clean. Cool in pans for 10 minutes, let cool completely on wire racks, these freeze well, too, or give a loaf to a friend.

PACK A PICNIC HONEY BREAD makes one loaf

New York produces gallons of maple syrup, but did you know that the state also produces a lot of honey? My sources say the yields of honey are just about half the production of maple syrup, and that is a lot of honey. The local beekeepers who produce all that honey are hard-working and friendly, the honey tastes wonderful, and a trip to a bee yard is truly a memorable experience.

2$^1/_2$ cups flour
2 teaspoons baking powder
$^1/_2$ teaspoon baking soda
1 teaspoon salt
2 tablespoons vegetable oil
1 egg
1 cup milk
$^3/_4$ cup honey
1$^1/_2$ teaspoons cinnamon

Preheat the oven to 350° and lightly grease a 9x5 inch loaf pan. Combine the dry ingredients and set aside.

In a mixing bowl, combine the vegetable oil and egg, stir in the milk, honey and cinnamon. Gradually add the dry ingredients, mixing well.

Pour batter into prepared pan and bake for 40 minutes. Remove immediately from pan and cool. This is very good picnic food, a slightly sweet bread that goes well with everything, and dense enough to pack well. If there any leftovers, toast some for breakfast and serve with cream cheese or butter.

OATMEAL DINNER ROLLS makes 18 rolls

2 cups water
1 cup quick cooking oats
3 tablespoons butter or margarine
1 package active dry yeast
$^1/_3$ cup warm water
$^1/_3$ cup packed light brown sugar
$1^1/_2$ teaspoons salt
$4^3/_4$ to $5^1/_4$ cups flour

In a saucepan, combine the 2 cups water, the oats and the butter; bring to a boil and boil, stirring, for one minute. Remove from heat and let cool to lukewarm.

In a large mixing bowl, combine the yeast and the warm water. Add the oat mixture, brown sugar, salt and 4 cups of flour and beat until smooth. Add enough remaining flour to form a soft dough. Turn dough onto a lightly floured board; knead until smooth and elastic, about 6 minutes. Add just enough flour to keep dough from sticking. Place in a greased bowl, turning dough over so the top is greased, cover with a towel and let rise until double, about 1 hour. Turn dough out onto a lightly floured board, spread into an even rectangle. Use a very sharp knife and cut the dough into 18 even pieces, shape into smooth balls.

Grease two 8 or 9 inch round cake pans, put 9 rolls into each pan, cover and let rise until double, 45 minutes.

Place rolls into a 350° oven, no need to preheat, and let bake for 25 minutes until golden brown.

Remove from the oven; remove immediately to wire racks to cool. These really are worth the effort, a hit with everyone who eats them.

SALADS AND SIDES

With the wide selection of fresh vegetables available, it has never been easier to vary your diet and reduce the intake of higher fat foods. All these recipes work well as 'sides' or try them for a light lunch or dinner. Make frequent visits to your local Farmer's Market, and you will soon be swapping recipes with the growers there. I have tried to select recipes that combine well with the main dishes in the book, so it is easy to mix and match a menu.

DILLED CUCUMBERS   serves 4

I always try to let some of my dill plants self seed in the fall and I watch for that tiny, feathery new growth in the spring. If I catch them while they are still less that 2 inches tall, I transplant them into a bed and let them grow. These will produce long before the direct seeded bed and will provide me with enough fresh dill for spring salads and chicken soup.

2 cups thinly sliced cucumbers
$^1/_2$ cup sour cream
2 teaspoons red wine vinegar
1 tablespoon honey
1 tablespoon chopped fresh chives
1 tablespoon chopped fresh dill

    Mix all the ingredients in a bowl, stir well and refrigerate until serving. This super easy salad is bursting with great spring flavor and makes a nice lunch all by itself.

EARLY SPRING PASTA WITH GARLIC serves 4

Asparagus is another sign of spring in the garden, I grow enough to feed us fresh and pick more at a local u-pick to freeze for winter. Combining asparagus with garlic makes a winning combination, the garlic cooks up sweet and flavorful.

2 tablespoons olive oil
12 spears fresh asparagus, cut on the diagonal into $^1/_2$ inch pieces
1 whole bulb garlic, each clove peeled and sliced, about $^1/_4$ cup
$^1/_4$ cup fresh parsley, chopped
$^1/_2$ cup white wine or chicken broth
Salt and pepper to taste
$^1/_2$ pound small bow tie pasta, cooked according to package and kept warm

In a large skillet, heat oil and add asparagus, cook over medium heat, stirring, for 2 or 3 minutes.

Add the garlic and parsley, continue cooking and stirring for 2 more minutes, add wine and salt and pepper, cover and let simmer for 2 more minutes. Serve at once over the hot pasta, tossing to coat. Other vegetables can be added to this, I usually add halved cherry tomatoes and some cooked shrimp for a main dish, quick and easy.

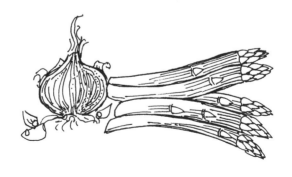

FOURTH OF JULY RICE serves 6

The combination of colors in this salad reminds me of fireworks, perfect as a summer celebration dish, easy to make ahead, too. Freeze any leftover rice until you have 4 cups, a great reason to make this salad.

4 cups cooked rice, white, brown or a combination
2 cups asparagus, cut on diagonal and steamed until crisp tender
$^{1}/_{2}$ cup sliced green onions
$^{1}/_{2}$ cup sliced radishes
$^{1}/_{2}$ cup chopped fresh tomato or halved cherry tomatoes
$^{1}/_{2}$ cup shelled fresh green peas
$^{1}/_{2}$ cup shredded carrot
$^{1}/_{2}$ cup mixed chopped fresh herbs, whatever you have or can get
(parsley, chives, lemon thyme, thyme, basil and dill)
Italian dressing, homemade or bottled
Fresh herb sprigs and edible flowers for garnish

Bring rice to room temperature and season with a small amount of dressing. Prepare the vegetables and herbs, combine with the rice and toss.

Refrigerate until serving time, just before serving add dressing to taste and garnish with herbs and flowers.

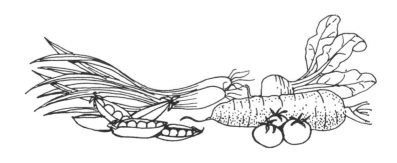

SUMMER TOMATO SALAD FOR 2

We wait a long time for fresh tomatoes, eating them warm from the garden is an experience not very many people get to enjoy. This salad is easy to double or triple to serve a whole crowd, for best flavor keep the tomatoes at room temperature.

2 tablespoons minced onion
1 teaspoon sugar
2 teaspoons water
1 teaspoon olive oil
1 teaspoon white rice vinegar
Salt and freshly ground pepper to taste
1 clove garlic, minced
1 or 2 fresh basil leaves, thinly sliced
2 medium red ripe tomatoes, sliced into $^1/_2$ inch slices

Combine the onion and the next six ingredients in a small bowl, stir well. Arrange the tomato slices on two plates, put sliced basil on top and drizzle with dressing. Serve with crusty bread and don't think about winter.

QUICK CHIVE POTATOES serves 6

We even freeze chives so we can have this dish all winter, just snip the clean chives, put them in reclosable plastic freezer bags and pop into the freezer. They stay green and fresh tasting for months.

6 medium sized potatoes
$^1/_2$ cup chopped chives
2 tablespoon olive oil
Salt and pepper to taste
1 tablespoon butter

Scrub and slice the potatoes, no need to peel them first. Slice them very thinly, using a mandolin or a very sharp knife.

Lightly grease a microwave safe baking dish and layer the potatoes, chives, salt and pepper and olive oil in 3 or 4 layers. Dot the top with butter and cover. Microwave on high power for 5 minutes, remove lid and stir gently, recover. Microwave for 5 or more minutes until potatoes are tender.

Serve hot. A tasty dish to complete hurried summer suppers.

SUMMER SQUASH SAUTE

Summer is busy, use the microwave oven to allow you to enjoy fresh vegetables prepared in a hurry. If a hike or a canoe trip kept you out of the kitchen, so much the better for you, keep this recipe handy for fast late night suppers.

$^1/_4$ cup butter
1 clove garlic, minced
1 tablespoon fresh oregano, or 1 teaspoon dried
2 or 3 fresh basil leaves
$^1/_2$ teaspoon salt
$^1/_8$ teaspoon pepper
2 small (5 inch) zucchini, thinly sliced
1 small yellow summer squash, thinly sliced
1 medium tomato, cut into 8 wedges

Place butter and garlic into microwave safe casserole. Microwave on high until butter is melted, about one minute. Mix in the herbs, salt and pepper, stir in zucchini and yellow squash, toss to coat. Cover and microwave on high until squash is tender, about 8 minutes, stirring after 4 minutes. Remove from oven and stir in tomato wedges, let stand, covered, for 2 minutes before serving.

ROASTED FALL VEGETABLES serves 6

A Farmer's Market favorite, this recipe is easily adaptable to what is available and what you like to eat. Experiment, adjust and enjoy.

1 small butternut squash, peeled and seeded, or any other winter squash
1 medium carrot
1 small rutabaga, softball sized, peeled
1 large potato
1 large red bell pepper, seeded
1 large red onion, peeled
A whole head of garlic, divided into cloves
     and peeled
1 tablespoon olive oil
Salt and pepper to taste
Three (3 inch) sprigs of fresh parsley
Three (3 inch) sprigs fresh thyme
3 or 4 sage leaves
Salt and pepper to taste

Vegetables fresh from the garden do not have the tough outer skin that comes from storage and exposure to the air. If the vegetables you are using are really fresh, you can skip peeling the carrot and potato, just scrub them well. Dice all the vegetables into 2 inch cubes or pieces and place in a large bowl. Add the garlic cloves. Sprinkle with the olive oil, salt and pepper and stir to coat.

Lightly grease a 9x13 inch pan and dump in the vegetables, spread the fresh herbs on the top.

Cover with foil and bake in a 450° oven for 30 minutes. Remove the foil, and continue to bake for another 5 minutes until vegetables are tender and slightly browned. This may seem like a lot of garlic, but that is the first vegetable to get scooped up and eaten, the roasting makes all the vegetables tender and sweet.

MAPLE BAKED BEANS serves 6

If you have time, start with dry beans and soak them overnight, drain and add fresh liquid and cook until tender. If not, the canned ones work well and save that extra step.

$^1/_4$ pound bacon
4 (15 ounce) cans navy or great northern beans, about 6 cups
1 cup maple syrup
1 teaspoon salt
$^1/_8$ teaspoon pepper
$^1/_2$ teaspoon dry mustard
1 teaspoon powdered ginger
2 slices bacon

Cook the $^1/_4$ pound bacon until crisp, drain and crumble. Place all ingredients except bacon slices into a 2 quart casserole or bean pot.

Stir well, and place the bacon strips in an 'x' on the top. Bake in a 250° oven for 2 hours, the slow cooking time really enhances the flavors. You can do this in the slow cooker, cook on low for 5 to 6 hours, but baking in the oven really results in the best dish, and a warm oven in the middle of February with great smells emerging is not a bad thing.

Soups, Chilis and Chowders

The Adirondack nights tend to be cool, even middle of the summer thunderstorms can drop the temperature rapidly. A steaming bowl of fragrant and satisfying soup, chili or chowder can be welcome at any time during all four seasons.

CREAMY SUMMER SOUP serves 4

This is a light summer soup, perfect for a first course or lunch, a great way to use some of that zucchini!

1 pound tender zucchini, washed and sliced, about 3 or 4 small zucchini
$^1/_2$ cup green onions, chopped
1 (10 $^1/_2$ ounce) can chicken broth
2 tablespoons chopped fresh basil
$^1/_2$ teaspoon dried thyme
$^1/_2$ teaspoon dried marjoram
Salt and pepper to taste
2 cups milk
Chopped green onion and basil leaves for garnish

In a saucepan, combine the zucchini, green onion, chicken broth, and herbs, bring to a boil. Reduce heat and simmer until zucchini is tender, 10 to 15 minutes, let cool.

Puree cooled zucchini mixture in a blender, return to saucepan, add the milk and season to taste with the salt and pepper. Heat gently, do not boil, serve when heated through, garnishing with chopped green onion or fresh basil leaves.

GARDEN FRESH TOMATO SOUP serves 4

Another light and creamy soup, perfect for late summer dinners in the garden, add some rolls or bread and a fruit dessert, relax, sit back and watch the fireflies.

4 medium ripe tomatoes, chopped
$^1/_2$ cup water
$^1/_2$ cup chopped onion
1 teaspoon sugar
$^1/_2$ cup chopped basil
$^1/_2$ cup chopped parsley
4 tablespoons butter
4 tablespoons flour
4 cups milk
Salt and pepper to taste

Simmer the tomatoes with the water, onion, sugar, basil and parsley over medium heat until the onions are tender, about 30 minutes.

Ladle this mixture into a strainer, pressing with a wooden spoon so some of the pulp comes through. Discard tomato skins and herbs, set the strained liquid aside. In a medium saucepan, melt the butter and add the flour, one tablespoon at a time, stirring after each addition until smooth. Slowly stir in the milk and cook until mixture is smooth and thick.

Add the tomato liquid slowly, stirring after each addition and allow to heat. Season with salt and pepper and serve when thoroughly heated.

PEASANT SOUP serves 6

Simple and satisfying, this easy soup comes straight from the garden.

3 ($10^1/_2$ ounce) cans chicken broth
1 cup water
4 medium onions, peeled
3 whole cloves
$^1/_4$ teaspoon pepper
$^1/_2$ teaspoon dried marjoram
$^1/_2$ teaspoon dried thyme
4 medium potatoes, peeled
$1^1/_2$ cups fresh green beans cut into 1 inch pieces
$^1/_2$ pound salt pork, in one piece

In a 4 quart Dutch oven or heavy saucepan, combine the chicken broth and 1 cup water.

Cut three onions into quarters, stud remaining onion with cloves and add them to the pot.

Season with the pepper and add the herbs. Bring to a boil, reduce heat, cover and simmer for 15 minutes. Slice the potatoes into thick ($^1/_2$ inch) slices; add to the chicken broth along with the beans. Bring back to a boil; reduce heat and simmer, covered, for 30 minutes. Meanwhile, dice the salt pork into $^1/_2$ inch cubes and brown in a skillet until crisp.

Drain off the grease and add to the soup, simmer 15 minutes more, serve with crusty French bread.

30

APRES SKI VEGETABLE SOUP serves 6

1 quart beef stock or beef broth
4 carrots, peeled and diced
4 medium potatoes, peeled and diced
2 onions, peeled and diced
2 stalks celery, diced
1 cup green beans, fresh or frozen
1 (6 ounce) can tomato paste
1 cup water
1 ($15^1/_2$ ounce) can great northern beans
Salt and pepper to taste

In a large soup pot, combine the beef stock with the carrot, potato, onion, celery, and green beans, cover and cook until vegetables are tender, about 40 minutes. Combine the tomato paste and water, stirring until smooth, and add to soup with the great northern beans and salt and pepper, stirring well to combine. Continue simmering until ready to serve. To do this in a slow cooker, combine all the ingredients in the cooker and cook on low for 10 hours or on high for 5 to 7 hours, this works well for cold, busy days, ready to serve whenever everyone is ready to eat.

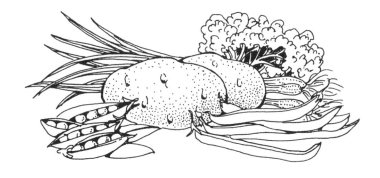

CREAM OF CAULIFLOWER SOUP serves 6

This is a rich, creamy soup, nice enough to serve to guests, but don't wait until company comes to try this recipe.

2 quarts chicken broth
2 pounds cauliflower, one medium head cut into 1 1/2 inch pieces
1 small onion
2 tablespoons butter
1 bay leaf
4 tablespoons butter
4 tablespoons flour
2 cups milk
2 cups cream
$^1/_2$ teaspoon salt
$^1/_4$ teaspoon white pepper

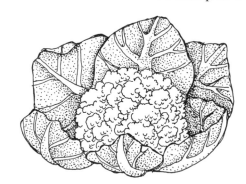

Heat the chicken broth in a large soup pot, add the cauliflower and cook until tender, about 15 minutes.

In a sauté pan, sauté the onion in the 2 tablespoons butter until translucent, add to the soup pot with the bay leaf. Continue to simmer, covered, over low heat.

Meanwhile, melt the butter in a small saucepan, stir in the flour one tablespoon at a time, stirring after each addition until smooth. Cook and stir for 10 minutes, do not allow it to brown. Add the flour mixture to the cauliflower mixture, bring slowly to a boil and cook until thick. Combine cream and milk, heat in a saucepan or the microwave, don't add cold milk to the soup or it may curdle. Stir the hot milk and cream mixture into the soup, remove the bay leaf, season with the salt and pepper and serve.

MOUNTAIN MINESTRONE serves 6

A hearty fall garden recipe, prepare the vegetables the night before, let it cook all day, go climb a mountain and come home hungry.

$^1/_4$ medium cabbage, shredded
1 onion, peeled and chopped
6 leaves Swiss chard, chopped
3 stalks celery, chopped
2 small potatoes, peeled and cubed
2 cups fresh tomatoes, peeled and chopped
1 small zucchini, cubed
1 (15$^1/_2$ ounce) can red kidney beans, drained
$^1/_4$ cup chopped fresh basil
2 tablespoons tomato paste
2 teaspoons salt
$^1/_4$ teaspoon pepper
Water to cover
Freshly grated Parmesan cheese

Combine all the ingredients except the cheese in the slow cooker crock, cover and refrigerate overnight. In the morning, place the crock in the slow cooker and turn to low, remembering to plug it in.

Let cook on low for 8 to 12 hours. Stir well before serving, ladle into bowls and top with Parmesan cheese.

33

CABIN FEVER CHILI serves 8 or more

Spicy and full flavored, there are no beans in this version of the ever popular chili. The combination of spices and herbs add just the right blend of heat.

$1/_4$ pound bacon, diced
2 lbs. beef chuck, cut into $1/_8$ in. pieces (do this in food processor)
2 medium onions, peeled and chopped
6 cloves garlic, peeled and minced
2 fresh jalapeno peppers, seeded and diced
1 (28 ounce) can whole tomatoes
1 (28 ounce) can tomato sauce
1 (12 ounce) can of beer
2 tablespoons chili powder
2 teaspoons ground cumin
1 teaspoon dried oregano
1 teaspoon Worcestershire sauce
1 teaspoon dry mustard powder
$3/_4$ teaspoon salt
$1/_2$ teaspoon paprika
$1/_2$ teaspoon red cayenne pepper
$1/_8$ teaspoon rubbed sage

    In a heavy Dutch oven or kettle, cook the bacon until crisp, add the meat, onions, garlic and chopped jalapenos. Stir and cook until the meat is browned and the onion is tender.

    Add the remaining ingredients and stir well. Cover and simmer for one hour or more, stirring occasionally. Check for seasoning, add more hot pepper, if desired, and serve.

MEATLESS 3 BEAN CHILI serves 8 or more

2 tablespoons vegetable oil
2 medium onions, peeled and chopped
3 cloves garlic, peeled and minced
2 (28 ounce) cans tomatoes
2 ($15^1/_2$ ounce) cans red kidney beans, do not drain
1 ($15^1/_2$ ounce) can black beans, do not drain
1 ($15^1/_2$ ounce) can garbanzo beans, do not drain
2 tablespoons chili powder
2 tablespoons hot pepper sauce
1 tablespoon ground cumin
1 teaspoon salt
$^1/_2$ teaspoon red cayenne pepper
Hot rice

Heat the oil in a large saucepan or Dutch oven. Add the onion and garlic, sauté until tender, about 5 minutes.

Stir in the remaining ingredients except the rice. Bring to a boil, reduce heat and simmer, covered for 30 minutes
Taste and adjust seasoning if necessary, serve over hot rice.

FISHERMAN'S CHOWDER serves 6

If the catch of the day didn't happen, substitute haddock or flounder from the store.

$1^{1}/_{2}$ lbs freshly caught fish; trout, pike, perch, sunfish or any combo
2 tablespoons olive oil
2 medium onions, peeled and chopped
2 medium carrots, peeled and diced
5 medium potatoes, peeled and diced
1 bay leaf
$^{1}/_{4}$ cup chopped fresh parsley
$^{1}/_{2}$ cup dry white wine
1 (8 ounce) bottle clam juice
1 cup water
1 teaspoon salt
$^{1}/_{4}$ teaspoon white pepper
4 cups scalded milk

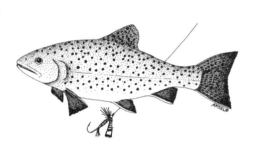

Clean and remove bones from fish, cut into one inch pieces and set aside. In a heavy soup pot, heat the oil and add the onions, sauté until tender, about 5 minutes. Add the carrot, potatoes, bay leaf, parsley, wine, clam juice and water.

Bring to a boil, reduce heat to a simmer, cover and cook for 35 to 40 minutes until potatoes and carrots are tender.

Using a potato masher, gently mash the soup until broth is creamy but mixture is still somewhat chunky.

Add the prepared fish and the salt and pepper, continue to simmer, covered, for 20 minutes, until fish is cooked.

Add the scaled milk; simmer for 15 more minutes, without boiling. Serve hot.

SMOKY CORN CHOWDER serves 6

$^1/_2$ pound bacon, diced
1 medium onion, peeled and chopped
1 red bell pepper, seeded and diced
1 stalk celery, diced
$^1/_2$ cup flour
2 cups chicken broth
3 medium ears of corn, husks and silk removed
2 medium potatoes, peeled and cubed
1 (15 ounce) can creamed corn
$1^1/_2$ cups milk
1 teaspoon salt
$^1/_4$ teaspoon pepper
Fresh chopped parsley for garnish

In a heavy soup kettle, cook the bacon until crisp, remove from pan and drain.

Remove all the bacon grease from the pan except about one tablespoon. Add the onion, bell pepper and celery, sauté in the bacon grease until tender.

Sprinkle the flour over the vegetables and continue to cook for one minute more. Slowly add the chicken broth, stirring to prevent lumps.

Bring to a boil; reduce heat to low and simmer, uncovered, until thickened. Cut the corn from the cobs and add to the soup with the potatoes, canned corn, milk, salt and pepper. Cook, uncovered for another 25 minutes or until potatoes are tender.

Ladle into bowls and garnish with fresh parsley.

Main Dishes

COUNTRY STYLE PORK WITH KRAUT serves 4

This is the best way to have sauerkraut, better than hot dogs or Reuben sandwiches. A wonderful combination of flavors that blend into a family favorite.

$1/_2$ pound bacon
2 pounds boneless shoulder cut pork steaks
3 cups sauerkraut, drained
3 apples, peeled, cored and thinly sliced
1 tablespoon brown sugar
1 teaspoon dried thyme
$1/_2$ teaspoon dry mustard
$1/_2$ teaspoon dried oregano
$1/_2$ teaspoon salt
$1/_2$ teaspoon pepper

In a heavy skillet, cook the bacon until crisp, remove from heat, drain and set aside.

Remove all the bacon drippings from the pan except one tablespoon; brown the pork steaks, one at a time in the bacon grease, doing both sides, until browned. Place the browned meat in a 9x13 in. baking dish.

Crumble the bacon and combine it with the sauerkraut, mix in the brown sugar, thyme, dry mustard, oregano and salt and pepper.

Arrange the sliced apples over the pork, spread the sauerkraut mixture over the apples and cover with foil. Bake in a 350° oven for one hour, or until pork is tender.

39

WILD RICE AND APPLE STUFFED PORK CHOPS
serves 6

6 rib pork chops, about one inch thick
$^1/_2$ cup cooked wild rice
$^1/_2$ cup unseasoned dry breadcrumbs
1 small onion, finely chopped
1 small stalk celery, finely chopped
1 small apple, peeled and chopped
1 egg, slightly beaten
1 tablespoon parsley flakes
1 teaspoon dried sage
$^1/_4$ teaspoon salt
$^1/_4$ teaspoon pepper
$^1/_2$ cup apple cider, apple juice or water

Trim the fat off the pork chops and, with a very sharp knife, cut a large gash or pocket into each pork chop, or have the butcher do this for you.

In a bowl, combine the remaining ingredients, except the $^1/_2$ cup liquid. Mix well to moisten and combine the ingredients. Fill the pockets with the dressing mixture and skewer with bamboo skewers if necessary, to keep them closed. In a large skillet, carefully brown the chops in a small amount of oil until browned on both sides. Put the browned chops into a covered ovenproof dish and add the cider, juice or water.

Bake in a 350° oven for one hour, checking occasionally and adding a bit more liquid to keep the chops from sticking to the pan.

MALONE MEAT PIES makes 2

This is a local adaptation of the French-Canadian tourtiere, a highly spiced meat pie that uses only pork. This version has been adjusted through the decades and is a common, but delicious addition to holiday meals throughout this region.

1 pound lean ground beef
1 pound lean ground pork
1 onion, peeled and minced
2 cups cold water
2 cups cracker crumbs (Saltines ground in
   the food processor)
$^1/_4$ teaspoon garlic salt
Salt and pepper to taste
1 beef bouillon cube
$^1/_2$ cup boiling water
Double recipe for a rich pie crust

   In a large bowl, mix the beef and pork together thoroughly. Combine the meat, onion and 2 cups water in a saucepan and bring to a boil.
   Boil for 10 minutes and let cool.
   Add the cracker crumbs, garlic salt, salt and pepper, mix well. Dissolve the bouillon cube in $^1/_2$ cup boiling water, add to the meat mixture.
   Line two 9 inch pie pans with pie crust, divide the meat mixture between the pans and top with remaining crust. Seal the edges well and cut slits in the top crust to let the steam escape. Bake at 350° for one hour. This is great to make in smaller pie pans for individual servings, and they freeze well, too.

SAVORY MEATLOAF

Adding horseradish to meatloaf may seem unusual, but I have several very old cookbooks that have similar recipes. Horseradish is easy to grow, and it certainly adds a spark to all dishes, this one will have everyone asking 'what is your secret ingredient?'.

2 pounds ground round steak
2 tablespoons prepared horseradish
1 (8 ounce) can tomato sauce, divided in half
1 teaspoon salt
$1/4$ teaspoon pepper
1 egg
1 tablespoon parsley flakes
1 medium onion, peeled and chopped
2 slices bread, cut into $1/2$ inch cubes
TOPPING:
2 tablespoon brown sugar
1 tablespoon prepared mustard
$1/2$ (8 ounce) can tomato sauce, reserved from meatloaf

In a large mixing bowl, combine the meat, horseradish, $1/2$ can tomato sauce (reserving other half for topping), salt, pepper, egg, parsley flakes, onion and bread.

Combine ingredients well, using a spoon or your hands. Lightly grease a 9x5 inch bread pan or an oven proof 2 quart casserole. Place the meat mixture into the prepared pan.

In a small bowl, combine the topping ingredients and spread evenly over the meatloaf.

Bake, uncovered, in a 350 degree oven for one hour. Remove from oven, let stand for 10 minutes and carefully remove from pan to serving platter so the topping remains on top. The best meatloaf ever for leftover meatloaf sandwiches.

CIDER BAKED HAM

A spectacular combination, a very special holiday main dish.

One 5 to 6 pound ham
2 cups apple cider, divided
$^1/_4$ cup soy sauce
2 tablespoons corn starch
1 tablespoon water

Preheat oven to 425°place ham, fat side up, on a large roasting pan and bake for 30 minutes.

Remove from oven and reduce heat to 325°. In a large bowl, combine $1^1/_2$ cups apple cider and the soy sauce and pour over the ham.

Cover and bake for 2 to 3 hours or until meat thermometer registers 160 degrees, basting with the juice frequently.

For the sauce, combine the remaining cider and the meat drippings in a pan. In a small bowl, stir the cornstarch into the water until smooth, stir this mixture gradually into the pan drippings and cider, cook and stir over medium heat for 12 to 15 minutes, until thickened.

Carve ham and serve with the sauce.

LAMB STEAKS WITH VEGETABLES serves 4

I really like lamb, but until recently, really fresh and nice looking lamb was hard to find in my local grocery store. Now, however, there are several local farmers' who are growing and selling lamb to the consumer, making it easier than ever to enjoy. If you can't find a local source, call your Cornell Cooperative extension agent, he or she will be glad to help.

4 shoulder lamb chops, 1 inch thick, about 2 pounds
2 tablespoons olive oil
1 cup celery, diced
1 large carrot, diced
3 medium onions, peeled and
   cut into sixths
$1^1/_2$ cup boiling water
2 chicken bouillon cubes
2 tablespoons tomato paste
2 tablespoons parsley flakes
2 tablespoons fresh lemon juice
1 cup fresh or frozen peas
Hot rice or noodles

    With a sharp knife, trim away the excess fat from the lamb chops.

    In a large skillet, brown the lamb chops in the oil on both sides, drain off all the grease.

    Dissolve the bouillon cubes in the boiling water and stir in the tomato paste. Put the prepared vegetables, reserving the peas, over the browned meat, pour the broth over all, sprinkle with the parsley flakes and lemon juice, cover and cook over medium low heat for 35 minutes. Add the peas, cover and cook for 5 minutes more or until meat is tender.

    Serve over hot rice or noodles.

GRILLED CHICKEN
WITH MAPLE MUSTARD GLAZE serves 4

Cooking out is a big part of an Adirondack summer, the smoke from the grill helps keep the black flies away, the food tastes delicious and the clean up is easy. This glaze is one of my all time favorites, use it on pork, beef and grilled vegetables, it works well on all of them.

1 broiler fryer chicken, cut into pieces
$1/_4$ cup maple syrup
3 tablespoons Dijon style mustard
2 teaspoons soy sauce
1 tablespoon fresh lemon juice
1 clove garlic, minced
$1/_2$ teaspoon black pepper

Cut away any excess fat on the chicken and place in a large, flat dish and refrigerate.

Combine the remaining ingredients in a saucepan and bring to a boil, boil for one minute, stirring.

Remove from the heat and brush both sides of the chicken with the mixture. Reserve remaining glaze. Cover chicken and refrigerate for one hour. Spray grill with non-stick cooking spray and heat until hot.

Grill the chicken over the hot coals, turning and basting frequently with glaze, until juice runs clear and chicken is no longer pink, about 30 to 40 minutes. This will also bake nicely in a 350° oven, baste frequently, and let cook for 15 minutes per side.

COOK OUT BEEF KABOBS makes 6

2 cups tomato juice
$1/2$ cup (1 stick) butter
$1/4$ cup finely minced onion
$1/3$ cup ketchup
1 teaspoon dry mustard
1 teaspoon salt
$1/2$ teaspoon paprika
$1/2$ teaspoon pepper
1 clove garlic, minced
1 tablespoon Worcestershire sauce
1 dash hot sauce
2 pounds beef sirloin, cut into 1 inch cubes
$1/2$ pound fresh mushrooms, stems removed
1 pint cherry tomatoes
1 large onion, peeled and cut into pieces
1 large red bell pepper, cut into 1 inch pieces

In a medium saucepan over low heat, combine the tomato juice, butter, onion, ketchup, mustard, salt, paprika, pepper, garlic, Worcestershire sauce and hot sauce, stir well. Simmer for 30 minutes, remove from heat and allow to cool. Brush the grill with oil and preheat to medium hot.

Place the beef cubes, mushrooms, tomatoes, onion pieces and bell pepper onto skewers as desired.

Brush all sides with the sauce and place on the grill. Grill for 10 to 15 minutes, occasionally turning and brushing with more sauce.

Serve this over hot rice or as a sandwich in thick slices of whole grain bread or pita bread, spooning extra sauce over each serving.

CHICKEN WITH HERB DUMPLINGS serves 4

2 tablespoons butter
2 boneless, skinless chicken breast halves cut into 1 inch cubes
1 medium carrot, diced
1 small onion, peeled and minced
1 clove garlic, minced
$1^1/_2$ cup sliced fresh mushrooms
1 cup fresh peas
2 cups chicken broth
2 tablespoons water
2 tablespoons cornstarch
DUMPLINGS:
$1^1/_2$ cups flour
3 teaspoons baking powder
$^1/_2$ teaspoon salt
$^1/_2$ teaspoon sage
1 tablespoon dried chives
1 cup milk

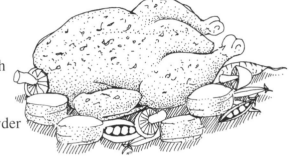

In a heavy skillet, heat the butter until it is melted, add the chicken and cook, stirring, until no longer pink, 3 to 4 minutes. Add the carrot, onion, and garlic, cook and stir 2 or 3 more minutes.

Stir in the mushrooms, peas and chicken broth, cover and simmer for 10 minutes. Stir the water and cornstarch together and add to the skillet, stirring over medium heat until thickened, 5 minutes or more. Prepare the dumplings by mixing the flour, baking powder, salt, sage and chives in a bowl.

Add the milk and mix until blended.

Drop the dumpling batter by rounded tablespoons onto the hot chicken mixture. Cover and cook over low heat for15 minutes without removing the lid.

Test the dumpling with a toothpick, cover and cook a few minutes longer, if necessary. Serve hot.

TRAIL'S END BEEF STEW serves 8

Made as a one pot slow cooker meal, this is a warming stew perfect after enjoying a day of outdoor activities.

3 pounds beef round or chuck steak, cut into 1 1/2 inch cubes
$^1/_3$ cup flour
1 teaspoon salt
$^1/_2$ teaspoon pepper
3 carrots, peeled, split lengthwise and cut in half
2 stalks celery, cut into one inch pieces
6 small white onions, peeled
6 to 8 small new potatoes, scrubbed
1 cup frozen or fresh green beans
1 cup frozen or fresh corn
1 (4 ounce) can mushroom slices
1 (10 $^1/_2$ ounce) can beef broth
$^1/_2$ cup dry red wine
2 teaspoons brown sugar
$^1/_4$ cup flour
$^1/_4$ cup water

Place the beef cubes in the slow cooker crock, combine the $^1/_3$ cup flour with the salt and pepper, and toss with the beef to coat. Add the vegetables and mix well. Combine the beef broth, red wine and brown sugar, add to crock. Cover and cook on low setting for 10 to14 hours or on high for 4 to 5$^1/_2$ hours.

Before serving, turn to high setting. Stir the flour and water to makes a smooth paste, add to stew and stir well. Cover and continue cooking until thickened.

Desserts

STRAWBERRY RHUBARB CAKE makes a 9x13 in. cake

This is a very old recipe which I have adapted for modern cooks, the dashes and pinches have been converted to real measurements, the great taste remains the same.

FILLING:
2 cups fresh tender rhubarb, diced
1 quart fresh strawberries,
  hulled and mashed
1 cup sugar
$1/_3$ cup cornstarch

TOPPING:
$1/_4$ cup ($1/_2$ stick) butter, melted
$3/_4$ cup flour
$3/_4$ cup packed brown sugar

CAKE:
3 cups flour
1 cup sugar
$1/_2$ cup (1 stick) butter
$1/_2$ cup shortening
1 teaspoon baking powder
1 teaspoon baking soda
$1/_2$ teaspoon salt
$1^1/_2$ cups buttermilk
2 eggs
1 teaspoon vanilla

Prepare the filling by combining the strawberries and rhubarb in a saucepan.

Cover and cook over medium low heat for 5 minutes. Mix the sugar and cornstarch and add to the saucepan, mix well, bring to a boil and cook, stirring constantly until thickened. Set aside to cool.

Prepare the cake by preheating the oven to 350°. In a large bowl, mix the flour, sugar, baking powder, baking soda, and salt, cut in the butter and shortening using a pastry cutter or your hands, until mixture is even and crumbly. Combine the buttermilk, eggs and vanilla; add to the flour mixture and mix to form a smooth batter. Spoon half the batter evenly into a lightly greased 9x13 inch pan, carefully spread the cooled filling over the batter, and drop remaining batter onto filling, trying to cover as much as possible. The filling will show through in several places, this is fine.

To make the topping, combine all the ingredients to make a crumbly streusel like mixture. Sprinkle this evenly over the cake and bake for 40 to 45 minutes. Cool in the pan and cut into squares. A rich and satisfying end to any springtime meal.

SUMMER BERRY CRISP serves 6

1 cup plus 1 tablespoon flour
1 1/2 cups sugar, divided
1 teaspoon baking powder
1/2 teaspoon salt
1 egg, beaten
5 to 6 cups mixed fresh berries, raspberries, blueberries, strawberries and/or blackberries
1/2 cup (1 stick) butter, melted

Preheat the oven to 350 degrees.

Combine 1 cup flour, 1 cup sugar, baking powder and salt in a bowl, stir to mix. Make a well in the center of the dry ingredients, add the egg and mix with a fork until crumbly, adding a few teaspoons of water if the mixture is too dry. Put the berries in a large bowl, add the remaining tablespoon of flour and 1/2 cup sugar, toss lightly to coat the berries.

Pour the berries in a lightly greased 2 quart oven proof casserole, sprinkle the flour mixture over the berries and drizzle with the melted butter. Bake for 40 minutes, until lightly browned, remove from oven, serve warm with cream or whipped cream, if desired.

WILD BLACKBERRY DUMPLINGS serves 6

It is an Adirondack tradition to gather wild blackberries, everyone has a favorite spot and comes home hot and sweaty, covered with scratches and bites, but convinced the adventure was well worth the effort. I can't argue with that, it really is worth the effort.

1 quart fresh blackberries, cleaned
1 cup sugar
$^1/_4$ teaspoon salt
$^1/_2$ teaspoon lemon extract

DUMPLINGS:
$1^1/_2$ cups flour
1 tablespoon sugar
$^1/_2$ teaspoon salt
2 teaspoons baking powder
$^1/_4$ teaspoon nutmeg
$^2/_3$ cup milk
Cream or whipped cream, to serve

In a heavy saucepan, combine the blackberries, 1 cup sugar, salt and lemon extract.

Bring slowly to a boil, reduce heat and simmer 5 minutes. In a mixing bowl, combine the flour, sugar, salt, baking powder and nutmeg, stir to blend well. Add the milk and stir until just blended. Drop by tablespoons onto the hot berries, cover tightly and simmer for 15 minutes, without removing the cover. A toothpick inserted into the dumplings should come out clean when dumplings are done.

Serve warm with cream or whipped cream.

EASY ALPINE APPLE CAKE makes a 9 inch square pan

I have been making this one for years; it always comes out perfectly, a handy recipe to serve to unexpected guests.

1 cup sugar
$^1/_4$ cup quick cooking oats
1 cup flour
$^1/_4$ cup shortening
$^1/_4$ cup cold water
1 egg
$^3/_4$ cup chunky applesauce,
    homemade or canned
$^3/_4$ teaspoon baking soda
$^3/_4$ teaspoon salt
$^1/_4$ teaspoon baking powder
$^1/_2$ teaspoon cinnamon
$^1/_2$ teaspoon nutmeg
$^1/_4$ teaspoon ground cloves

Preheat oven to 350°. Generously grease a 9x9 inch baking pan. Measure all ingredients into a large mixer bowl. Blend on low speed for one minute, scrape down sides of bowl, and increase mixer speed to medium high, beat for $2^1/_2$ minutes more, scraping bowl twice more.

Pour batter into prepared pan and bake for 50 minutes or until center of cake springs back when gently pressed.

Remove from oven and cool, in pan, on wire rack. We don't ever frost this; it is good as is, nice for breakfast on the go, too.

MAPLE SUGAR PIE

This recipe is probably one of the oldest recipes I have, another traditional Adirondack recipe made every spring during sugar season.

$^1/_2$ cup (1 stick) butter, melted
$^1/_2$ cup packed light brown sugar
1 cup real maple syrup
3 eggs
1 tablespoon flour
$^1/_8$ teaspoon salt
1 teaspoon vanilla
$1^1/_2$ cup pecan halves or other nuts (optional)
1 unbaked 9 inch pie shell

Preheat the oven to 425°. In a saucepan, melt the butter with the brown sugar, stir in the maple syrup, eggs, flour, salt and vanilla.

Beat until well combined, fold in the nuts, if using, pour into unbaked pie shell, and bake for 10 minutes. Reduce oven heat to 375° and bake for 35 minutes until center is puffy and mixture is set.

Chill before serving.

This is a sweet Valentine's Day recipe, try doing it in tart pans, topping the mixture with the nuts rather than stirring them in and bake these at 325° for 40 minutes.

ADIRONDACK SNOW PIE

This is a summer pie, a new tradition for the Adirondack baker.

1 cup flour
$^1/_2$ cup toasted and chopped almonds
$^1/_4$ cup packed brown sugar
$^1/_2$ teaspoon cinnamon
$^1/_2$ cup (1 stick) butter, melted
2 egg whites
$^1/_4$ cup sugar
$^1/_2$ gallon raspberry ice cream, softened
$^1/_4$ cup raspberry syrup
Fresh raspberries for garnish

In a medium bowl, combine the flour, almonds, brown sugar, and cinnamon, toss to mix. Stir in the melted butter and mix well. Press this mixture into a lightly greased 9 inch pie pan and bake in a 350° oven for 8 to 10 minutes, until lightly browned. Remove from oven and allow to cool completely.

Preheat broiler.

In a small mixing bowl, beat the egg whites until frothy. Gradually beat in the sugar until stiff peaks form.

Spread the softened ice cream in the cooled pie shell. Cover the top of the pie with the stiff egg whites, spreading right to the edges to seal; this prevents the meringue from shrinking. Make mountain peaks in the meringue using a dull knife, place under the broiler and watch closely, remove from oven when meringue starts to turn golden.

To serve, cut pie into pieces, put onto dessert plates and drizzle with raspberry sauce and fresh raspberries.

UPSIDE DOWN GINGER CAKE   serves 8

Not a gingerbread at all, but a delicate ginger flavored dessert, absolutely delicious!

3 tablespoons butter
$^1/_2$ cup maple syrup
3 ripe pears, peeled, cored and halved
1$^1/_2$ cups flour
2 teaspoons baking powder
2 teaspoons powdered ginger
$^1/_2$ teaspoon salt
$^1/_2$ cup (1 stick) butter
$^1/_2$ cup sugar
$^1/_2$ cup milk
1 egg
Whipped cream, if desired

Preheat the oven to 375°. In a small pan, melt 3 tablespoons butter and stir in the maple syrup. Lightly grease the sides of a 9 inch round cake pan, pour the butter mixture into the pan. Arrange the pear halves in a nice design in the pan. Mix the flour, baking powder, ginger, and salt, set aside.

Melt 1 stick of butter in a saucepan, remove from the heat and stir in the sugar, beat well. Add the milk and egg, and beat until well combined.

Add to the flour mixture and beat until smooth. Carefully pour the batter over the pears and bake for 25 to 30 minutes, until a wooden toothpick tests clean. Remove from the oven, cool in the pan for 10 minutes. Place a serving plate over the cake pan and invert the whole thing, holding both together firmly. If the topping is not arranged to your liking, you can gently rearrange it while the cake is still warm.

Serve warm with whipped cream, if desired.

MAPLE GINGERBREAD serves 8

Much different than the preceding recipe, hearty and spicy, this is fall food at its finest.

1 cup maple syrup
1 cup sour cream
1 egg, well beaten
$2^1/_3$ cups flour
2 teaspoons baking soda
$1^1/_2$ teaspoons ginger
1 teaspoon cinnamon
$^1/_2$ teaspoon ground cloves
$^1/_2$ teaspoon salt
4 tablespoons vegetable oil

Preheat oven to 350° Combine the maple syrup, sour cream and egg, beat well. Stir together the dry ingredients and add to the syrup mixture, beating well to combine, stir in the vegetable oil. Lightly grease a 9x9 inch square baking pan, pour in the batter and bake for 30 to 35 minutes, or until wooden toothpick tests clean.

Remove from oven, let cool in pan for 10 minutes, remove from pan to a wire rack, serve warm with ice cream or take it with you on a hike.

TRAIL MIX OATMEAL COOKIES makes about 2 dozen

A necessary food addition to any outdoor activity, these are one of my favorite cookies.

$1/4$ cup ($1/2$ stick) butter, softened
$1/4$ cup shortening
$1/2$ cup firmly packed brown sugar
$1/4$ cup sugar
1 egg
1 tablespoon water
$1/2$ teaspoon baking soda
$3/4$ cup flour
$1/2$ teaspoon salt
$1/2$ teaspoon vanilla
$1 1/2$ cups quick cooking oatmeal
$1/2$ cup sweetened coconut
1 cup semisweet chocolate chips
$1/3$ cup dry roasted peanuts
$1/2$ cup raisins

Preheat the oven to 375° and lightly grease 2 cookie sheets.

In a mixer bowl, combine the butter, shortening, brown sugar, and white sugar, beat until light. Add the egg and water and mix. Stir in the baking soda, flour, salt and vanilla. Add the remaining ingredients and mix until combined. Spoon rounded tablespoons onto cookie sheet, and use the back of the spoon to gently press the dough into a 3 inch circle.

Put 12 cookies on each sheet, spacing them evenly. Bake for 8 to 10 minutes, until lightly browned, remove with a spatula to wire racks and let cool completely. Store in airtight containers, they will keep up to a week.

UP NORTH SHORTBREAD makes 3 dozen cookies

1 pound (4 sticks) butter, softened
1$^1/_2$ cup packed light brown sugar
$^1/_4$ cup maple syrup
4$^1/_2$ cups flour

Preheat the oven to 350°. Combine the butter, brown sugar, and maple syrup, beat until light. Add the flour and mix until a smooth dough is formed.

On a lightly floured surface, roll the dough $^1/_2$ inch thick and cut with cookie cutters, I use a maple leaf for this, but any shape is fine, place on un-greased cookie sheets.

Bake for 20 minutes until very lightly browned, do not over-cook or they will be tough. Cool completely on wire racks and store in air-tight containers.

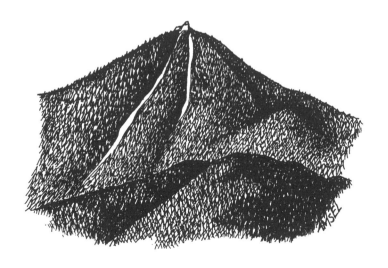

Gifts From the Kitchen

One of my favorite things to do is to make some special treats to share with others who do not garden, or cook, or live in the Adirondacks.

A gift of food from your own home really does show the recipient how special they are to the giver, and everyone loves to receive a tasteful gift from the kitchen.

PRESERVED STRAWBERRIES

makes 4 (8 ounce) jars

My dream is to gather enough wild strawberries to make this recipe, it would really be impressive, and those tiny wild strawberries would look beautiful in the clear orange liquid. Until that happens, I use perfect, small strawberries from my berry patch.

$1^{1}/_{2}$ quarts small, ripe strawberries
$1^{1}/_{2}$ cups sugar
4 (1 inch) cinnamon sticks
2 cups Grand Marnier liqueur, more if necessary

Carefully clean and hull the strawberries. Combine them with the sugar in a bowl, toss gently to coat. Wash 4 (8 oz) jars, I use jelly jars but any decorative jars work fine, rinse well and drain. Carefully fill each jar with the sugared berries, taking care not to crush the berries, place 1 cinnamon stick into each jar. Pour the Grand Marnier over the berries to cover.

Tightly seal and store in refrigerator for one month before using. Serve on pound cake or ice cream, these have a shelf life of 6 months.

BLUEBERRY SYRUP makes 3 pints

2 quarts ripe blueberries, cleaned, washed and drained
2 cups water
1 tablespoon grated lemon peel
3 cups sugar
4 cups water
2 tablespoons fresh lemon juice

In a large saucepan, crush the blueberries with a masher or the bottom of a heavy mug.

Add the 2 cups water and lemon peel, bring almost to a boil, reduce heat and simmer for 15 minutes.

Let cool slightly.

Drain through several layers of dampened cheesecloth or jelly bag, squeezing to extract the juice and some of the pulp. This will stain your hands, so wear gloves.

Mix the sugar and 4 cups water, bring to a boil and boil for 15 minutes, or until syrup is clear, reduce heat and stir in blueberry juice and lemon juice. Mix well to combine and let heat thoroughly. Ladle into clean glass jars, let cool, cap tightly and store in the refrigerator.

Use this syrup within a month of making, you can substitute frozen berries for the fresh and enjoy this year round.

A delicious treat on waffles, pancakes or ice cream.

CHIVE BLOSSOM VINEGAR makes 2 quarts

The chives in my garden flower pretty much before anything else. I use the delicately onion flavored flowers in salads, scrambled eggs and for this favorite herbal vinegar.

1 quart chive blossoms
2 quarts white wine vinegar
1 (1 gallon) glass jar
Plastic wrap
Decorative corked jars
Fresh chives

Pick the chive blossoms into a large flat container, I use a roasting pan. Shake the pan to spread blossoms evenly and place in a shaded location for 30 minutes. This allows any insect friends to leave on their own, my no work method for cleaning herbs.

Pick over the flowers to remove any other debris and wash gently, drain well. Place them into the clean gallon jar, and put the jar onto a folded dish towel. Heat the vinegar until just below the boiling point; it will be just starting to steam.

Pour the hot vinegar over the chives and cover the jar with plastic wrap. Let this stand for at least 12 hours, the vinegar will turn a really pretty pink as it takes on the essence of the chive blossoms. Clean the bottles you will be using and put a few fresh chives into each one. Strain the vinegar and ladle into the decorative jars, cork tightly.

Use this in salad dressings and marinades, or, of course, as gifts.

RHUBARB CHUTNEY makes 4 pints

Serve chutneys with grilled meats or as a condiment with any meal, or serve a dish with a cheese and bread plate. No one will guess this isn't a high priced version from a specialty food store, it's that good!

$3^1/_2$ pounds rhubarb, cut into 1 inch pieces
3 cups sugar
1 pound raisins
2 large oranges, peeled, sectioned and cut into
one inch pieces
1 cup cider vinegar
1 cinnamon stick
6 whole cloves

Combine rhubarb, sugar, raisins, oranges and vinegar in a large saucepan.

Tie the cinnamon stick and cloves into a square of cheesecloth and push into the rhubarb.

Cook over low heat, stirring frequently until rhubarb is soft and mixture is thickened.

Remove from heat, remove spice bag and ladle into 4 clean pint jars, adjust caps. Process this for 10 minutes in a boiling water bath, if desired, or store in refrigerator until ready to use or give away. If you keep your rhubarb well picked and watered, it will stay tender for most of the summer, so you can make batches of this as necessary.

HONEY NUT POPCORN

Easier to make and not as sweet as caramel corn, keep this in mind for thoughtful trick or treats.

$^1/_2$ cup honey
$^1/_2$ cup butter
$^1/_2$ cup salted mixed nuts
3 quarts popped popcorn

Melt the honey and butter together. Remove any un-popped kernels from the popcorn, stir in the mixed nuts.

Pour the honey/butter mixture over the popcorn and mix well until nuts and popcorn are evenly coated. Spread onto 2 cookie sheets and bake in a 325° oven for 20 minutes, stirring frequently.

Remove from oven, let cool, and break into pieces and bag in cellophane bags. Tie with season appropriate ribbon and share with friends.

SPICED HONEY makes 3 cups

Cold weather always heralds the start of sniffle season, use this flavorful honey in hot tea for a quick pick me up, or serve it on toast and waffles.

3 cups honey
One lemon, sliced and seeded
12 whole cloves
3 (3 inch) cinnamon sticks
3 clean (8 oz) jars

Slice the lemon into 6 slices; stick 2 cloves into each slice. Put the honey, lemon slices and cinnamon sticks into a saucepan and heat until boiling, stirring occasionally. Remove from heat.

Place 2 lemon slices and one cinnamon stick into each jar, pour the hot honey into each jar, cap tightly.

A very easy and thoughtful fall gift, pair this with some gourmet herbal teabags and a special mug for a memorable teacher present.

SWEET CIDER JELLY makes 10 (8 ounce) jars

I looked for this recipe for years, finally I found it in an old, out of print Canadian cookbook, I made some adjustments and now this is one of my favorite jellies.

6 cups sweet apple cider
7 cups sugar
3 (3 inch) cinnamon sticks
1 (1.75 oz) package powdered pectin
10 (8 oz) jelly jars

Wash the jelly jars and let them stand in hot water until ready to use. Put the jelly jar lids into a small saucepan, bring to a boil, reduce heat and let simmer gently until ready to use. Measure the sugar into a large bowl and set aside. In a large, heavy saucepan, combine the cider, pectin and cinnamon sticks.

Bring to a full, hard boil and add the sugar, all at once. Stirring constantly, bring mixture back to a full boil and boil for one minute.

Remove from heat; discard cinnamon sticks and skim off any foam. Remove jars and jar lids from water, ladle or pour hot cider mix into jars, and cap tightly.

You can process these in a boiling water bath for 10 minutes and they will keep for at least one year, or store the jars in the refrigerator and use within 3 months.

MULLED CIDER MIX makes 6

We love hot spiced cider, so I make a bunch of these easy spice packets to have handy for cider season. Give one to someone with a gallon of cider; they will love it, too.

12 (one inch) cinnamon sticks
6 teaspoons whole cloves
6 teaspoons whole allspice
3 chamomile teabags, opened or 3 teaspoons loose chamomile flowers
2 bay leaves, crumbled
6 (5 in.) squares washed unbleached muslin
White string to tie bags

Place 2 cinnamon sticks, $^1/_2$ teaspoon cloves, and $^1/_2$ teaspoon allspice onto each square of fabric.

Divide remaining ingredients evenly between the squares, fold corners up and tie with string.

To make the cider, place one gallon of cider into a large kettle or slow cooker, add one spice bag, heat gently for one hour or more. Serve warm with another cinnamon stick to stir. I always make this one gallon at a time, then cool the leftovers, store in the refrigerator and re-heat in the microwave, a nice breakfast beverage.

CHOW CHOW FOR NOW makes 8 cups

An 'end of the garden season recipe', this slightly spicy relish makes either a tasty condiment or side dish, great with grilled steak or on hot dogs.

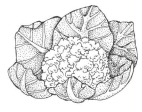

2 cups cider vinegar
$^1/_2$ cup sugar
$^3/_4$ teaspoon black pepper
2 teaspoons salt
$2^1/_2$ teaspoons dry mustard
1 cup cauliflower, trimmed and cut into small pieces
1 cup cabbage, cut into small cubes
1 ear fresh corn, cut from cob, about one cup
1 cup diced red bell pepper
1 cup diced green bell pepper
1 cup diced sweet red onion
2 ribs celery, diced

Combine the vinegar, sugar, black pepper, salt and dry mustard in a large, heavy saucepan. Bring to a boil over medium high heat and stir in the cauliflower, cabbage, corn, red and green bell pepper, onion and celery. Bring to a boil, remove from heat and allow to cool.

This is ready to eat immediately, store in the refrigerator until ready to use, or give away. I save any decorative glass jars I get and use them to package fresh food gifts, top with a square of colorful fabric and a twine tie for a nice thank you gift.

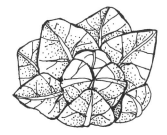  

MAPLE GRANOLA makes 7 cups

Use this as a breakfast cereal, a trail mix or a snack, a favorite with all.

3 cups rolled oats
$1^1/_2$ cups wheat germ
1 cup coarsely chopped almonds
1 cup flaked coconut
1 cup hulled sunflower seeds
$^1/_2$ cup sesame seeds
$^1/_2$ cup vegetable oil
$^1/_2$ cup maple syrup
$^1/_2$ cup raisins
$^1/_2$ cup chopped apricots

In a 9x13 inch baking pan, combine the oats, wheat germ, almonds, coconut, sunflower seeds and sesame seeds.

Place in a 350° oven and toast, stirring occasionally, for 15 minutes. In a small saucepan, combine the vegetable oil and maple syrup, heat gently until hot, pour over toasted ingredients and stir well to coat evenly.

Return to oven, continuing to toast and stir occasionally, for 15 to 20 minutes, until lightly browned.

Remove from oven, let cool, stir in the raisins and apricot pieces, store in airtight containers.

About the Author...

Wendy Harrington is the creator and owner of Harvest Herb Company in Malone, New York, selling culinary herb and spice blends since 1983. Her weekly recipe column in the "Malone Telegram" focuses on cooking with local ingredients. She is an active member of the Adirondack Farmer's Market Cooperative, has judged the produce at the Franklin County Fair and grows an abundance of herbs, vegetables and flowers in her upstate zone 4 garden.

About the Illustrator...

Sheri Amsel is the author and illustrator of over 20 books. With a lifelong interest in nature and outdoor education, her work can be found in libraries, schools, bookstores and nature centers throughout New York and the U.S. www.adirondackillustrator.com.